LeTTeRS

from

GoD

for children

What Matters Publishing House

IVAN TAIT

Published by
What Matters Publishing House
PO Box 62820, Colorado Springs, CO 80962

International Standard Book Number (ISBN)   978-9893060-4-1

Design and Layout: What Matters Ministries and Missions
Printed in South Korea.

I dedicate this book to my children: Bethany, Kindra, Gavin, Caden, Judah and Abbi. You fill the hollow places of my heart with wonder and love.

Introduction

There is no greater reward than seeing our children truly blessed. They have the power to open our hearts to unreached treasures. Their triumphs cause celebration, their achievements awe, and so, as parents, we must train our children in the way of Godly victory. They will fight battles, feel pain, struggle to understand, be tempted, and experience the suffering of a fallen world. Whether they go from strength to strength and glory to glory is initially dependent upon their parents.

You are God's first line of defense, His first source of blessing. You are His protection and His voice. Before they can read, you are quite literally the Word of God for your children. This is parenting God's way.

Letters from God for Children is a parent-child journey that will knit your hearts together. It is a cozy fire to snuggle by. It is a flotation device for parents who may be struggling to connect. It is a compass for parents and children needing God's direction, and it will strengthen families and navigate them through the rocks that others have crashed upon.

You will have the opportunity to have creative, God-inspired interactions with the hearts of your children. The anatomy of the parent-child relationship will change as you shift into a mentor's role. The influences of peers, media, and threatening voices will dwindle, and you will be equipped to nurture the fertile places of their souls, heal brokenness, and redirect any rebellion.

Along their journey, many children begin to struggle with identity, security, esteem issues, and hidden hurts. These feelings can manifest through disobedience, aggression, lying, rebellion, or closing up and withdrawing. Any loving parent who is concerned with the spiritual well-being of their children will recognize these behaviors as the warnings they are. Parents are the guardians of their child's spirit and must have access to it. *Letters from God for Children* will keep the hidden heart chambers open and help to open ones that have been sealed shut. Bad seeds will be uprooted, and God will use you to plant truth in their place.

This is not a "how to" book. It is a God-breathed invitation into parenting as He intended it. Answers to your child's questions will be revealed. You will find yourself teaching your son or daughter spiritual truths that will equip him or her for God's great purposes. They will flourish as they begin to understand mercy, purpose, faith, love, power, purity, security, and the many facets of God.

This may just be the greatest tool a parent could receive for reaching into their child's heart and pulling out the God-destiny that was written there.

Walking with *Letters from God for Children*

PRACTICE REPETITION
You will see that each entry contains a theme, a focus verse, a letter, a memory verse, and seven discussion questions (one for each day). *Letters from God for Children* is designed for each letter to be read and reread for a whole week. I believe that this repetition is necessary for both deepening the hearts of your children and allowing them

the time to process the revelations and form whatever questions may arise.

MEMORIZE THE WORD
Each day they will have a chance to go over the memory verse and by the end of the week they will have retained it. Your child has a spirit and that spirit needs the Word of God to fill it. The foundation of God's Word is what sets His people apart and keeps them in His will.

PROTECT FROM HARM
Please protect your children. Guard against individuals, TV-shows, movies, and your own behaviors that could hurt their spirits. As parents, we all must ask ourselves this question: when our children leave our home, are they more or less equipped to serve God? Did we partner with God or work against Him? If you apply yourself to the daily routine that *Letters from God for Children* creates, you will confidently answer "yes" to having partnered with God in the protecting and releasing of your children's spirits.

PARTNER WITH GOD
Pray over this time of discipleship and remember: your children are the blessing of God. He has great purposes for them and has entrusted them to you. He will equip you, fill you, and reveal new understanding to you. His Holy Spirit will be active in your times together. Stay humble, stay patient, stay reverent, and enjoy being involved in the miraculous work of the God Who cherishes your children.

Connect Children to orphans

TRAIN YOUR CHILDREN'S HEARTS

You can:

1. Connect them with our orphans and their stories,

2. Pray blessings and purpose over a new orphan each day (as a breakfast or bedtime routine),

3. Knit your children's hearts to God's as you read our orphans' stories and discuss the great purposes God must have for them,

4. Train your children in selflessness as they begin to care for orphans and widows.

Pure and genuine religion in the sight of God the Father means caring for orphans and widows in their distress and refusing to let the world corrupt you.

James 1:27, NLT

Go to WhatMattersMM.org and click SEE THE CHANGE

Growing into Your Shoes

And the boy Samuel continued to grow in stature and in favor with the Lord and with people.

—1 Samuel 2:26, NIV

I made you the way you are, without any flaws or mistakes. The growing pains just mean you are growing into your shoes. Know that My love for you is perfect! And you fit into My heart perfectly, because there is no one like you. You are My special, perfect child, so I made you a pair of special shoes. They hold the secrets to your future; therefore, I am teaching you how to grow into and walk in them. They will protect you from the dangerous roads of life and keep you safe from the harms outside. Love these destiny-shoes. They know where to take you, and they will always lead you back to Me! Now grow into your shoes!

Memory Verse

The path of the righteous is like the morning sun, shining ever brighter till the full light of day.

—Proverbs 4:18, NIV

Discussion Questions

1. What does it mean to be on a journey?

2. How can I trust God to lead me on the right path?

3. In what ways does God direct my journey?

4. Who are people God has given me to help me in my journey?

5. Who is one person God directed/led in the Bible?

6. How can I grow more and more into my destiny-shoes?

7. How do my destiny-shoes protect me?

You're My Garden

The Lord will always lead you.
He will satisfy your needs in dry lands.
He will give strength to your bones.
You will be like a garden that has much water.
You will be like a spring that never runs dry.

—Isaiah 58:11

I will be there when you need Me most. You see, you're My garden. I have already planted the destiny-seeds that will help grow the roots, the trees, and the fruits of your life. None of your fruit will spoil or be stolen; no infected words are allowed to grow in you. No foxes can steal your grapes or spoil your vines. You are My garden; I care for you and will always protect you from anyone who tries to steal any part of Me from any part of you. I am here now with you. Sleep in the perfect peace of a seed! Now close your eyes, and grow into Me.

Memory Verse

You will be secure, because there is hope;
you will look about you and take your rest in safety.

—Job 11:18, NIV

Discussion Questions

1. What is security?

2. What are the blessings of being secure?

3. How does fruit spoil?

4. How do I develop security?

5. What are destiny-seeds?

6. What things threaten security?

7. Why do I need security?

WK3: PEACE
The Angels' Wings

He has put his angels in charge of you.
They will watch over you wherever you go.

—Psalm 91:11

When you sleep, My angels stay awake; they stand over you, covering you with their wings—you are always safe in their care! You never have to fear anything in the dark; My angels never sleep, day or night. Their job is to keep you safe! And their wings reach from wall to wall. They help you grow and become great. You're so special to Me that I will always make sure you're alright. Enjoy every day! Grow your heart and water your mind with obedience. Your family is your fruit tree; they also will be there to see you become a world-changer. Everything you need I have already provided, including all of your friends, all of your journeys, all of your adventures along the way, and everything you do! The angels' wings are there covering, protecting, and watching out for you. So rest, forgive, say goodbye to yesterday's pain, and put your arms around Me—I already have Mine around you. Now grow into your angel wings.

Memory Verse

Those who love your teachings will find true peace.
Nothing will defeat them.

—Psalm 119:165

Discussion Questions

1. What is peace?

_____

_____

2. Where do I find peace?

_____

_____

3. How do I say goodbye to yesterday's pain?

_____

_____

4. How does my family help me to produce fruit?

_____

_____

5. Who had peace in the Bible?

_____

_____

6. How does peace guide me?

_____

_____

7. How do I give peace?

_____

_____

WK4: ADVENTURE
up to the Mountaintop

He said unto Simon, "Launch out into the deep."
—Luke 5:4, KJV

You were designed for discovering mysteries that no one else has ever known. I am going to take you to the mountaintops of life. No dry, painful places for you, because you will have the greatest life, with the greatest people—and the most wonderful fun! Time is Mine, and I have planned some adventures for us in it. I am the Creator of all the mountains in the entire world, places where you can go on great adventures and learn the mysteries of Divine power and life-changing truth. In these places, your feet can stand on the mountaintops of My Presence. Oh My child, get ready for the most fun life you could ever have. I will unfold your adventures like the unfolding of a tablecloth. "Climb higher!" is your shout. Jump into the mysteries that are Me. When you're at the top, you can see the whole world clearly! So grow into your mountain-climbing shoes!

Memory Verse

In your strength I can crush an army;
with my God I can scale any wall.

—Psalm 18:29, NLT

Discussion Questions

1. What is "adventure"?

_____

_____

2. How do I live in the adventure of God?

_____

_____

3. Why should I be adventurous?

_____

_____

4. What are the blessings of an adventurous life?

_____

_____

5. How is life an adventure with God?

_____

_____

6. What are some of God's best mysteries?

_____

_____

7. Discuss your favorite Bible adventure.

_____

_____

Your Heart, My Hiding Place

You are my refuge and my shield;
your word is my source of hope.

—Psalm 119:114, NLT

My hiding place is your heart. I have made My home there—that's why you are never far from home! You are a walking miracle of love and kindness, infinitely valuable. When others are rude, you are kind; when they are hard, you are soft. You get this when you make Me your Hiding Place, where you learn to love others. You get this because your value comes from Me, Who I am, and who you are in Me. Every time you return a blessing to them, I lend a blessing to you. You will never be alone, unwanted, or displaced. Your heart is My home, and I am happy there. Smile all night, when you dream or when you wake up. I am your Perfect Hiding Place, but never forget, you are also Mine! You don't have to go anywhere to find Me. I am already within you, and your heart is the perfect, warm place for Me. I love living there; it's My favorite resting place. There I can see everything you need, hear everything you feel, and fix everything that hurts. Always welcome Me in your heart and I will never leave! Now grow into your Hiding Place.

Memory Verse

For you are my hiding place;
you protect me from trouble.
You surround me with songs of victory.

—Psalm 32:7, NLT

Discussion Questions

1. What is "value"?

_____

_____

2. Why does God value me?

_____

_____

3. How do I make God my Hiding Place?

_____

_____

4. What are the blessings of knowing my value?

_____

_____

5. Why should I value others?

_____

_____

6. How do I find my value?

_____

_____

7. How do I return blessings when others are rude? Why?

_____

_____

WK6: PURPOSE
Use Your Shield

After these things happened, the Lord spoke His word to Abram in a vision. God said, "Abram, don't be afraid. I will defend you. And I will give you a great reward."

—Genesis 15:1

I have handmade a special power-shield just for you. Nothing bad can penetrate your shield; it is made of pieces of Me. Faith, love, purity, wisdom and truth: these are the special ingredients of your faith-shield should someone throw a spear of hurtful words at you. My shield will deflect it. Those words will fall to the ground without ever hurting you because My shield has been in many battles and never lost. Hurtful words will try to steal your purpose, but My shield knows no defeat and cannot fail. It was designed just for you—so use it! Keep it with you at all times. Never leave it at home when you go to battle; it will protect you and My purpose for you, keeping you safe. It is your shield made by Me so that you can be My champion! This shield is yours—now grow into it.

Memory Verse

You protect me with your saving shield.
You have stooped to make me great.

—2 Samuel 22:36

Discussion Questions

1. What is "purpose"?

2. How do I use my shield?

3. How do I find my purpose?

4. What are the blessings of purpose?

5. How are spears thrown at me?

6. What are the thieves of purpose?

7. What is my shield made of?

Your Superpower God

Jesus stood up and commanded the wind and the waves to stop. He said, "Quiet! Be still!" Then the wind stopped, and the lake became calm.

—Mark 4:39

Do you know that I am equipped with superpowers that no one else has? I can walk on water or through walls, I can make it rain frogs, and I can see into your heart. I can part the oceans and fashion the stars. Yes, I can heal the sick and open deaf ears. I am your superpower God; no one has superpowers like Me. I made the world. I can stop a storm with one word, I can speak to angels, and only I can make the sun stand still. I make the trees clap their hands. I tell animals to speak, and they do. I tear the ground open, and I'm the one who makes birds sing. I am your Superpower God. I make the flowers bloom and the hummingbirds fly. I am so powerful that the whole universe has to obey Me. Everything everywhere does what I say. I can raise the dead. I can even make a fish bring Me money and change rocks into bread. Only I can change a heart. I am your Superpower God. All the superpowers are just for you. Whenever you need them, I will weave them into your life until you become My superpower child. Embrace who I am and what I can do. There will be no end to your superpower life! Now grow into all of it.

Memory Verse

I tell you the truth. He who believes in Me will do the same things that I do. He will do even greater things than these because I am going to the Father.

—John 14:12

Discussion Questions

1. How am I equipped?

_____

_____

2. Why do I need equipping?

_____

_____

3. Discuss some of these miracles.

_____

_____

4. What are the blessings of being equipped?

_____

_____

5. What people were equipped in the Bible?

_____

_____

6. How does God change a heart?

_____

_____

7. Why does being unequipped produce fear?

_____

_____

WK8: FAITH

Would You Like to Walk on Water with Me?

Peter said, "Lord, if that is really you, then tell me to come to you on the water." Jesus said, "Come." And Peter left the boat and walked on the water to Jesus.

—Matthew 14:28-29

Would you like to walk on water with Me? I am the God of the impossible and I have created you to do impossible things. You will not face a no-miracle life. I will always teach you what I know. You're a water-walker now—no sinking, no gasping for air, no drowning in a panic. Peace is yours. Strength is your middle name, skill is your gift, and I am your destination. Never doubt what I am able to do through you. Standing in what I have prepared for you makes you amazing. When you walk on water with Me, you'll want to show the whole world how to walk on water with us. There will be no boring days for you—only dancing, laughing, and singing in victory. Get ready; the water is calling, and I'm already here waiting for you. Put on your water-walking shoes and let's go where you've never been before!

Memory Verse

Without faith no one can please God. Anyone who comes to God must believe that He is real and that He rewards those who truly want to find him.

—Hebrews 11:6

Discussion Questions

1. What is faith?

_____

_____

2. How do I grow in faith?

_____

_____

3. How does faith please God?

_____

_____

4. In my life, what does water represent?

_____

_____

5. How do I live by faith?

_____

_____

6. What are the blessings of faith?

_____

_____

7. How do I walk on my water?

_____

_____

Safe in My Arms

Look, the Lord God is coming with power. He will use his power to rule all the people. Look, he will bring reward for his people. He will have their payment with him.

—Isaiah 40:10

Safe is a good word; it is a happy word. Believe Me that he or she who is safe is happy, and that I carry you in My invisible arms. Nothing bad can reach you there; you are beyond the reach of evil people, places, and things. My arms are the safest place on earth, and they are all yours. Every day you can be safe in My arms if you pray to Me. I reach out to you if you praise Me. I pick you up if you worship Me. I wrap My arms around you; that's how I work. Worship is how you let Me keep your heart, your soul, and your spirit safe from painful words and hurtful individuals. Thanksgiving releases My arms to hold you far away from any damage to your soul and spirit when you trust Me with them. I squeeze you with love when you obey, and I celebrate and design your future as you trust Me. And when you are kind, I form the shape of your heart. No danger is allowed in your life. Stay always in My arms. Learn how to walk embraced and live surrounded by My arms. I am your Safe Place!

Memory Verse

The everlasting God is your place of safety. His arms will hold you up forever...

—Deuteronomy 33:27

Discussion Questions

1. What is fearlessness?

_____

_____

2. Am I afraid of anything?

_____

_____

3. What is the cure to fear?

_____

_____

4. Why is fear bad?

_____

_____

5. How does God carry me?

_____

_____

6. How does fear steal from me?

_____

_____

7. What are the blessings of fearlessness?

_____

_____

The Songs They Sing in Heaven

"Our Lord and God! You are worthy to receive glory and honor and power. You made all things. Everything existed and was made because you wanted it."

—Revelation 4:11

The songs they sing in Heaven are about Me and about you. Angels play their instruments when you pray. When you sing, everyone in Heaven begins to clap and dance! I will give you these songs as you grow. And new songs will come—some will come while you're sleeping, some will come while you're playing, and still others will come while you're walking with Me, listening to My voice and learning the melodies of My heart. Here in Heaven, they already sing the songs you're going to write. Your songs will make the sick world well. They will know the tears of the weeping heart of the world. They will bring joy to those walking in sadness. They will heal the brokenhearted. Your songs will be like a paintbrush, with every stroke painting a new part of My face. Love will surround your songs and joy will be their echoes. These are the songs they sing in Heaven. I already wrote them, and now I give them to you so that you can heal the world!

Memory Verse

I will sing to the LORD as long as I live. I will praise my God to my last breath!

—Psalm 104:33, NLT

Discussion Questions

1. What is worship?

_____

_____

2. What does worship do?

_____

_____

3. What are the blessings of worshiping God?

_____

_____

4. How do I worship God each day?

_____

_____

5. Who in the Bible had a worshipful spirit?

_____

_____

6. Why is it important to sing to God?

_____

_____

7. What is something you can worship God for today?

_____

_____

My Shoulders Are Big Enough for You

*...Let the beloved of the Lord rest secure in him,
for He shields him all day long, and the one the Lord loves
rests between His shoulders.*

—Deuteronomy 33:12, NIV

My shoulders are as big as mountains, and on them you can stand with strength. You see, I've made you to fit perfectly on My shoulders. From this place, there is no problem you cannot solve and no height you cannot reach. As you grow taller and stronger, always remember that I am taller and stronger still; I am your high-mountain God. You were made for seeing life from on top of My shoulders. I am so strong that nothing can reach you when you're standing on My shoulders. I will carry you there all your life. Whenever you're not sure where you're going, climb back on My shoulders where you can see clearly. I will always pick you up. I am higher than the birds than the moon or stars. My shoulders have no equal; anyone who stands on them becomes as tall as I am, as powerful as I am, and as unreachable as I am. There is no safer place for you, My child, than My shoulders. Come on, climb up—see the world as I do. It's great up here! I have amazing things for you. You were made to climb the heights of My will for your life!

Memory Verse

Then the Lord answered me and said:
"Write the vision
And make it plain on tablets,
That he may run who reads it."

—Habakkuk 2:2, NKJV

Discussion Questions

1. What is vision?

2. How do I develop vision?

3. What are the blessings of seeing from God's shoulders?

4. Who had vision in the Bible?

5. Why does God give me a vision?

6. What happens when people lose vision?

7. When feeling sad, how do I climb on God's shoulders?

Sleeping in My Cocoon

Jesus grew in wisdom and in stature and in favor with God and all the people.

—Luke 2:52, NLT

Never feel bad about yourself. Why? Because I know something you don't know about change: every worm is not a worm—it's a future butterfly. When you make a mistake and feel bad, stop yourself, and think, "I am not a worm; I'm just crawling on my way to my Heavenly cocoon. Yes, in there I will sleep inside of my Father's love. Each day I spend in His cocoon, I'm growing and changing and becoming a beautiful butterfly. I will have strong wings that will lift me high above the dirt and the mud and the predators of the world." You see, no one hates a butterfly, no one. Butterflies are gentle, kind, and harmless. They simply represent the beauty of your Heavenly Father, and that's what you're going to do. Your cocoon is truly amazing because it changes you ever more into a beautiful creature. Don't fear the cocoon; it is healing, secure, and warm. The cold of life cannot reach you there! In your cocoon, the other cruel creatures cannot step on you. There you are safe and able to change. Oh, get ready My child! Something stunning is happening to you. Soon you will emerge and fly into your destiny—high, high into the skies! Make everyone remember: if I did it for you, I can do it for them!

Memory Verse

Don't copy the behavior and customs of this world, but let God transform you into a new person by changing the way you think...

—Romans 12:2, NLT

Discussion Questions

1. How does God develop me?

_____

_____

2. How do I stay in God's cocoon?

_____

_____

3. What are the blessings of development?

_____

_____

4. Why do I need to let God develop me?

_____

_____

5. How can I stop feeling like just a worm?

_____

_____

6. What is God developing in me?

_____

_____

7. Discuss how something can be developed every day.

_____

_____

The Mighty Rock

My God is my rock. I can run to him for safety. He is my shield and my saving strength. The Lord is my high tower and my place of safety. The Lord saves me from those who want to harm me.

—2 Samuel 22:3

There is a Rock where all wise travelers hide. No storm can sweep you away from there, no flood can drown you, and no lightning can hurt you. I protect those inside the Rock, and they are safe. Yes, this Rock has a name. What is Its name, you ask? Jesus, The Rock of Ages. He alone can keep you from life's troubles; this Rock is your hiding place. No tornado, no hurricane, no thunder can reach you—you are safe, protected, and kept inside this Mighty Rock. This Rock is always there even if you cannot see Him. He's your Rock when you pray. The Rock is your shelter when you sleep, and He gets even bigger—The Rock protects My children; He has saved My lost and wondering souls. Come, stay close to Me—never go into a storm or ride the waves without Me! Live close to Me and I will always stay close to you, covering you. I have decided to always take care of you, both now and for all your life. Your name is now etched in the Rock! Be like Jesus, the Mighty Rock, for greatness awaits those who are!

Memory Verse

He is the Rock, his works are perfect, and all his ways are just.
A faithful God who does no wrong, upright and just is he.

—Deuteronomy 32:4, NIV

Discussion Questions

1. What is greatness?

_____

_____

2. Who was great in the Bible?

_____

_____

3. In what ways is God great?

_____

_____

4. Why do I need to be great in God?

_____

_____

5. How does God keep me from future trouble?

_____

_____

6. How does greatness bless God?

_____

_____

7. How do I make others great?

_____

_____

W K 1 4 :   D E S T I N Y

Take My Hand and Never Let Go

I am with you, and I will protect you everywhere you go. And I will bring you back to this land. I will not leave you until I have done what I have promised you.

—Genesis 28:15

I am your Heavenly Father. I love you so much that I cannot stand one day without you. Take My hand and let Me show you everything I've created and how I created it. I made the lion with his roar, the bear with his claws, the eagle with her wings, and the horse with his mane. I love everything and everyone perfectly; I can never hurt or harm anyone. I am only Love, never hurt. I don't like anyone to be hurting, suffering, or feeling alone. When you feel misunderstood, take My hand. When you feel afraid, place your palm in Mine, and I will love the fear away. When you're lost, I will light the path back to Me. You're Mine forever, and I will never leave you, nor forsake you. See, I am incapable of losing you or forgetting you; I will never do it. Not ever, ever, ever! I will never let go of you. My hand pulls you into My love, and My love is like glue between us; it's how I keep us connected. From it come healing, wholeness, and peace. My hand can create anything you need, always and forever. I will hold you close to Me. Trust My hand and you'll never get lost. Together we will unravel your destiny!

Memory Verse

Your arm has great power.
Your hand is strong. Your right hand is lifted up.

—**Psalm 89:13**

Discussion Questions

1. What is destiny?

2. How does God reveal my destiny?

3. How do I pursue my destiny?

4. What can I find in God's hand?

5. What is the power of a destiny?

6. What things hinder destiny?

7. How do I take God's hand when I am afraid?

I Am Watching Over You!

The Lord says, "If someone loves me, I will save him. I will protect those who know me. They will call to me, and I will answer them. I will be with them in trouble. I will rescue them and honor them. I will give them a long, full life. They will see how I can save."

—Psalm 91:14-16

I am watching over you everywhere that you go. There is no place you can go where I will not be with you. I protect you whether you're on a plane or in a car, if you're swimming or running. I am watching over you—I am your personal bodyguard. I am the best protector in the entire universe. After all, I am stronger than everyone in the world put together—who is stronger than I am or more powerful?

I am Power; I am Strength. Yes, every day I am your power and strength. I am making you stronger as I watch over you. I will always take care of you because I love you. I will turn your dark night into daylight, and I will even keep you from hurting yourself. I will keep you free from every danger. No broken bones, no broken heart, no broken dreams—I will not allow them. Walk with Me, love Me, follow Me, serve Me, and I will watch over you. I am your Heart's Song, your Mender and Healer—I am your total Joy. I make you laugh and enjoy every single day to its fullest. Like the sweetness of grapes, so I will make your life dance. I'm always watching over you. Trust Me from this moment on, and I will also watch over everyone you love—always!

Memory Verse

But the Lord is faithful. He will give you strength and protect you from the Evil One.

—2 Thessalonians 3:3

Discussion Questions

1. What is protection?

_____

_____

2. Where do I find protection?

_____

_____

3. How do I protect others?

_____

_____

4. How can people be unprotected?

_____

_____

5. How does God make me stronger?

_____

_____

6. Who were people in the Bible that were protected?

_____

_____

7. Why is God Power and Strength?

_____

_____

Hiding Inside the Ark

*And Noah and his sons and his wife and his sons' wives entered the
ark to escape the waters of the flood.*
—**Genesis 7:7, NIV**

Noah was very smart, just like you. He never questioned My wisdom.
He knew the safest place on Earth is inside My will. So when he
built the ark for himself and his family and all the animals, he never
doubted that I would make it float. He never said, "Oh no! What if it
sinks?" He knew Me; he knew My voice and he knew I would never
let him sink. Every animal was safe, every single creature I would use
to start a new world was safe, and so was Noah. Remember all your
life that the safest place is always inside My will. The Ark won't help
people not in it—the storms and thunder and lightning are outside
the Ark, not inside. You see, all your life, whatever you do, wherever
you go, look for My Ark, My safe place—look for My will. That's
where you'll always find Me. That is where you will find your peace,
your rest, and your joy. Nothing dangerous can find you inside My
will. I will show you over and over, any time you need, where to find
My ark. So when you're not sure, ask yourself, "Where is the ark?
Where is my Father's will?" Seek out this safe haven and I will show it
to you. I love you too much to keep you in darkness! Now close your
eyes and go to sleep, safe inside the ark!

Memory Verse

Trust the Lord with all your heart. Don't depend on your own understanding. Remember the Lord in everything you do. And he will give you success.

—Proverbs 3:5-6

Discussion Questions

1. What does the ark mean for me today?

_____

_____

2. Why do I need to trust?

_____

_____

3. Why do I need to be trusted?

_____

_____

4. How does God make me trustworthy?

_____

_____

5. How is the safest place for me in God's will?

_____

_____

6. How do I find God's will?

_____

_____

7. Who were people that were trusted in the Bible?

_____

_____

Your Superpowers Are Coming

And those who believe will be able to do these things as proof: They will use my name to force demons out of people. They will speak in languages they never learned. They will pick up snakes without being hurt. And they will drink poison without being hurt. They will touch the sick, and the sick will be healed.

—Mark 16:17-18

As you read My Word and learn from Me, your superpowers will grow. Just as I can walk on water, heal the sick, and restore a broken heart, so you, too, will have superpowers. These are My gifts to you— to give them to those who have no one, who are loved by no one, and wanted by no one. Your superpowers will make the brokenhearted well and cure the sorrows of others' souls. They will make you strong when others are weak. They will make you feel the invisible needs of others. You will sense when their hearts are crying, and you will have My power to wipe those tears away. Your superpowers come from Me; they are specifically made for you to change the world. I will give you any superpower you need. Should you need to know the answer to a problem, you will have it. The cure for loneliness—yes, you have that. There will be a parade of miracles following you all your life. With My superpower living inside you, the world's offerings will be unnecessary; I will be enough. You'll never live without answers and solutions because I am your superpower!

Memory Verse

But the Holy Spirit will come to you. Then you will receive power. You will be My witnesses.

—Acts 1:8

Discussion Questions

1. How do I grow superpowers?

_____

_____

2. Why am I unique?

_____

_____

3. Why do I need the power of God?

_____

_____

4. What happens when we become unique?

_____

_____

5. Does everyone have access to this power? Why not?

_____

_____

6. How is God unique?

_____

_____

7. Who was power-filled in the Bible?

_____

_____

WK18: AFFIRMATION

You're Never in Trouble with Me!

"With a little wrath I hid My face from you for a moment;
But with everlasting kindness I will have mercy on you,"
Says the Lord, your Redeemer.
—Isaiah 54:8, NKJV

I already know how wonderful you are—you see, I made you with no flaws. Your potential is My gift to you. When you're in trouble, and you feel low or bad or angry, look up to Me and remember that you're never in trouble with Me. Know that I love you and that I know your heart is good. I made it, so I know that with Me you'll be alright. I am your special Handyman—there is nothing broken that I cannot fix. I can make everything work again; all your life this will hold true. If it's broken, bring it to Me. Even if *you* broke it, still bring it to Me. You're never in trouble with Me. I know every mistake you will ever make, and I know beforehand how to fix it. Before it breaks, I've already seen how I will fix it. That means you need to live large; dream, laugh, run, enjoy life, and be an explorer of it! I will never be mad at you. I love you every day, all day, with an everlasting love. Very few people can love this way, but I do, because you're never in trouble with Me. So shine like the stars!

Memory Verse

God sent his Son into the world not to judge the world, but to save the world through him.
—John 3:17, NLT

Discussion Questions

1. What is affirmation?

_____

_____

2. Why do I need affirmation?

_____

_____

3. How do I affirm others?

_____

_____

4. What are the blessings of affirmation?

_____

_____

5. Who were people that were affirmed in the Bible?

_____

_____

6. Why am I never in trouble with God?

_____

_____

7. What does God say about me?

_____

_____

The Land with No Fear

I asked the Lord for help, and he answered me.
He saved me from all that I feared.

—Psalm 34:4

Fear is a mind-monster—if you fix your mind, you cure your fears. Never be afraid of anything or anyone, because you live in the Land with No Fear. Where is that, you ask? That place is the arms of My heart, the place where I live, inside of you. In the Land with No Fear, you are bold, strong, courageous, and unintimidated. Fear always runs away from the Truth. Fear hates The Light because fear cannot grow near it. Fear can only grow in a garden of lies, but it must disappear in a garden of love. Learn to love everyone and everything, and you will never fear. Fear is not your food; it is the sound of lies talking. I declare over you that you will be fearless and powerful, full of wisdom, truth, strength, and amazing talent. There shall be no fear following you around. You are now faith-filled and fear-proof. Go ahead and live your adventures—with no fear of anything!

Memory Verse

For God has not given us a spirit of fear and timidity, but of power, love, and self-discipline.

—2 Timothy 1:7, NLT

Discussion Questions

1. What is boldness?

_____

_____

2. Who was bold in the Bible?

_____

_____

3. How can I be bold?

_____

_____

4. Why is the Devil afraid of bold people?

_____

_____

5. What happens when I am bold?

_____

_____

6. How do I fix my mind?

_____

_____

7. Discuss why God loves people being bold.

_____

_____

This Is What My Face Looks Like

God once said, "Let the light shine out of the darkness!" And this is the same God who made his light shine in our hearts. He gave us light by letting us know the glory of God that is in the face of Christ.

—2 Corinthians 4:6

My face is in the sound of a baby laughing, a mother kissing her son or daughter, a father playing with his children, and a Savior dying on the cross to save everyone. My face is found in telling the truth when you don't want to and giving love to those who don't like you. My face is praying for those that treat you rudely and try to hurt you. My face is found in a forgiving heart and a gentle answer. My face is you loving your family, and most importantly, My face is taking care of the elderly, loving orphans, helping the poor, and providing for widows when they need help. It is My face to bless those who curse you—and freedom also is My face. It is anywhere love walks, talks, or smiles. I am everywhere if people will look, and you will never have to live without seeing My face. I will always reveal My face to you when you look for Me. Love forgives, heals the sick, comforts the sorrowful, and mends the brokenhearted. This is My face shining out of you!

Memory Verse

Because I have lived right, I will see your face.
When I wake up, I will see your likeness and be satisfied.

—Psalm 17:15

Discussion Questions

1. Where do I see God's face?

_____

_____

2. Why does God want to be intimate with me?

_____

_____

3. How can God's face shine out of me?

_____

_____

4. How is looking at someone's face intimate?

_____

_____

5. What happens when we grow distant?

_____

_____

6. How can I pray intimate prayers?

_____

_____

7. Why does God love intimacy?

_____

_____

My Paintbrush

The Lord directs the steps of the godly.
He delights in every detail of their lives.

—Psalm 37:23, NLT

Your future will be made up of all the amazing colors of Heaven. You see, I use love colors to paint your future. Some only use darkness as their color, but not Me. I use red for forgiveness, blue for Heaven, yellow for joy, white for purity, and green for life. Yes, I am painting your future with the colors of the rainbow. Every color is a virtue. Every shade is an adventure I will lead you on. I will paint your life with My love-paintbrush. No gray, no gloom, and no ugliness are in your future. Get ready for your color life! I will paint wonder, beauty, success, wisdom, contentment, strength, might, and understanding into your heart and mind. Every color I add to your life etches a piece of Me into it. I am not dull or dim, nothing like a shadow. I am clear and bright and light! I reflect diversity. You see, I made everyone in the whole world of beautiful color—all different, all equal, and all unique. Embrace every color in your life. Never fear new color, for your future depends on it. Now sit back and watch Me paint your color-life with My love-paintbrush!

Memory Verse

For we are God's masterpiece. He has created us anew in Christ Jesus, so we can do the good things he planned for us long ago.

—Ephesians 2:10, NLT

Discussion Questions

1. How can I have a colorful life?

2. How can I be creative?

3. How do new colors come into my life?

4. What are the blessings of creativity?

5. What is the best way to become creative?

6. Discuss how God is a Creator.

7. Discuss how/why to never shy away from creativity.

WK22: WORTHINESS

How Much Are You Worth to Me?

You will be like a beautiful crown in the Lord's hand.
You will be like a king's crown in your God's hand.

—Isaiah 62:3

You are so important to Me that I gave up everything I love most to rescue you for My sake. I am full of love for you. You are worth more than the stars, the sky, even the universe. All the treasures in the entire world mean nothing to Me compared to you. I never want to be away from you. I never want to spend one day without you, My child. Oh, how I love you! All day every day I am thinking about how I can bless you, make you happy, and make all of your dreams come true. I always take perfect care of you, and I am always on your side; everything I am belongs to you now. I have made you My favorite child of grace. Never doubt this! Never believe the liars that would question that you are My favorite. They are wrong. You are the best, with no flaws, no ugliness, and no lack of being amazing. I created you, My Son died for you, and I resurrected Him for you. I already have all you need. Nothing will ever be missing from you. I have dedicated Myself to you for your entire life. Every day you will discover a new piece of My love for you. Drink it, eat it, and become it—because I love you!

Memory Verse

For God loved the world so much that He gave His only Son. God gave
His Son so that whoever believes in Him may not be lost,
but have eternal life.

—John 3:16

Discussion Questions

1. What is worthiness?

_____

_____

2. Why does God never want to be away from me?

_____

_____

3. How does God make me worthy?

_____

_____

4. What am I worth?

_____

_____

5. How do I discover more of God's love for me?

_____

_____

6. How does knowing my worth protect me?

_____

_____

7. Can I lose my worthiness?

_____

_____

WK23: PERSPECTIVE
On Eagles' Wings

"You yourselves have seen what I did to Egypt, and how I carried you on eagles' wings and brought you to Myself."

—Exodus 19:4, NIV

I have placed you on eagles' wings; with Me you fly—no crawling, no gasping for air, and no barely surviving. With Me, you fly. I know that sometimes people want to drag you down and make you feel inferior, but come to Me and I will lift you up and put you on eagles' wings. I will lift your spirits up above storms so you can soar with the eagles. You see, eagles can soar above the troubles of the lower world where rats and snakes crawl. Eagles' wings can catch the wind currents and sore effortlessly into the arms of freedom. Yes, freedom: that's the destination for you, where you will be free from everything bad that has ever happened to you. I will free you from any rat or snake or spider that has ever done anything to scare you. High, higher, and to the highest you will climb. Life will be a soaring victory for you as long as you ride on My eagles' wings. I never planned for you to drop or fall or fail. There is no failure for you, no stumbling in the dark. Rise up! Look up, take hold; the ride of your life is about to begin!

Memory Verse

But those who trust in the Lord will find new strength. They will soar high on wings like eagles. They will run and not grow weary. They will walk and not faint.

—Isaiah 40:31, NLT

Discussion Questions

1. What is perspective?

2. Why do I need perspective?

3. What is God's perspective?

4. What are wrong perspectives?

5. How do I ride on eagles' wings?

6. What are the blessings of perspective?

7. How does God see me?

WK24: DIVINE HEALTH
I Am Your Doctor

Lord, my God, I prayed to you.
And you healed me.

—Psalm 30:2

No sickness can survive around Me. I am Medicine, I am Health, and I am Inner Strength. One word from Me and germs die, viruses flee, diseases dissolve, and wounds disappear. I am your Personal Doctor! I live to heal your wounds and remove the dirty fingerprints of life. I am The Cure. I am The Solution. As The Remedy for life, I cannot and will not leave you sick. I will restore every part of you until you are perfectly whole in My sight. Never will you be crippled or weak. I am the perfect Health Doctor. I know every cure for every ailment; one beautiful prescription cures it all. Know that you are worth keeping healthy. You are worth a home visit. Did you know that I make house calls? Expect them when you pray. Wherever you are is home to Me—because you are My home. I promise I will cure everything in your life, forever. No trouble will grow, no sorrow will thrive, and no ailment will celebrate any victories over you, ever. Open your heart wide and drink in My healing medicines of love, joy, and peace!

Memory Verse

Let all that I am praise the Lord; may I never forget the good things he does for me. He forgives all my sins and heals all my diseases.

—Psalm 103:2-3, NLT

Discussion Questions

1. What does it mean to have God as your Personal Doctor?

2. In what ways can I choose to live healthily?

3. What does it mean to live in divine health?

4. Who did Jesus heal in the Bible?

5. Discuss how there is power in the Word of God.

6. Why does God promise to heal me?

7. Are there any wounds in my heart that need healing?

WK25: ASSURANCE

I Will Walk Through Walls to Find You!

That Sunday evening the disciples were meeting behind locked doors because they were afraid of the Jewish leaders. Suddenly, Jesus was standing there among them! "Peace be with you," he said.

—John 20:19, NLT

There is no place you can be that I will not find you. I will walk through walls to find you if I have to. You'll never be hidden from Me. Never, for one moment, will you be out of My sight. No one can hide you from Me, not one person, sin, fear, doubt, or trouble. If you can't find Me, then I will find you. I see everything, everywhere, all the time. You are never out of My sight. Never are you lost from Me. I am your Deliverer, your Rescuer, your Safe Harbor. Don't ever worry; you will never lose Me. I have engraved your place in My heart, your name on My mind, and your location in My hands. Be happy with where you are, who you are, where you're going, and trust My life-map. It knows where you should turn and when you should go straight. There are no lost places on your life-map. My love has planned every place. So surrender, follow, and trust, because I will walk through walls to find you!

Memory Verse

But the eyes of the Lord are on those who fear him,
on those whose hope is in his unfailing love.

—Psalm 33:18, NIV

Discussion Questions

1. What is assurance?

_____

_____

2. How can I be assured?

_____

_____

3. Which people in the Bible had assurance?

_____

_____

4. What are some habits that grow assurance?

_____

_____

5. Why should I trust God's life-map?

_____

_____

6. What are the blessings of assurance?

_____

_____

7. How can I be assured God will never let me out of His sight?

_____

_____

WK26: DIRECTION
I Am Your Pilot

Let the morning bring me word of your unfailing love, for I have put my trust in you. Show me the way I should go, for to you I entrust my life.
—Psalm 143:8, NIV

Have you seen the birds fly and how they never get lost? They know, without being told, where to go and are never confused about their directions. They can leave their nests and always find their way back home. That's because I am their inner pilot, and I am never lost. I know everything, and I am everywhere at the same time. There are no hidden places with Me, no secret places where bad people can hide. Like the birds, I have put My Holy Spirit in you, and I will be your Life-Pilot. I will guide you into all truth and lead you to your favorite places. I will never steer you wrong or lead you to dark and cold lands. I lead you to where I live, to where life grows, and to where peace blossoms and sadness dies! Yes, I lead you to where your heart can grow and heal. I lead you to the destiny places of life. Never fear where I am taking you; be like the birds and fly into your journey. Trust My Holy Spirit in you. Go where I go, stay where I stay, leave when I leave, and you will always land on your feet. Always be where I am—only then can you be as happy as I am. Now spread your wings and fly with Me!

Memory Verse

*The Lord says, "I will make you wise. I will show you where to go.
I will guide you and watch over you."*

—Psalm 32:8

Discussion Questions

1. What is "direction"?

2. How do I listen to my Life-Pilot?

3. In what ways does God lead me?

4. Who were people that had direction in the Bible?

5. How do I trust the Holy Spirit in me?

6. Where does God direct people?

7. Who does God lead?

WK27: DESTINATION

Something Special in the Stars for You

You will teach me God's way to live.
Being with you will fill me with joy.
At your right hand I will find pleasure forever.

—Psalm 16:11

Every star I made has a name. Yes, every single one. There are numberless stars, and each star is special to Me. Each star can light up a universe. Each star is a world of its own. I made you like the stars. You will shine in life; you will stand out for Me. You are a universe of gifts, potential, and discoveries. Like the stars, you will light up the world with My truth, music, and power. You will lead the blind into the light. You will shine inside My glory; you will give direction to the wandering ships in the world. You were created to reflect the light I put inside you. Every gift is a light. Every truth you tell turns on a light for someone. Every virtue you live up to is a reflection of freedom for the captive slaves. You are My shining star, My bright giver of truth; you are My reflection of true life. In you there is no darkness, no dimness, and no weakness; you are a bright and shining light. Light up your world and shake the Earth with truth. Expel the darkness. Replace the dark fog with great clarity! Give away your light and I will give you more. Cover the earth with the light of My Word and I will be your Star!

Memory Verse

Let your light shine before others, that they may see your good deeds and glorify your Father in heaven.

—Matthew 5:16, NIV

Discussion Questions

1. What does it mean to have a destination?

_____

_____

2. What is my destination?

_____

_____

3. How do I reflect the light God put inside me?

_____

_____

4. How am I a "universe of gifts and potential"?

_____

_____

5. What are the blessings of seeking a destination?

_____

_____

6. How does God lead me to my destination?

_____

_____

7. Why do I need a destination?

_____

_____

Growing God-Muscles

There was a long war between the people who supported Saul's family and those who supported David's family. The supporters of David's family became stronger and stronger. And the supporters of Saul's family became weaker and weaker.

—2 Samuel 3:1

Weakness is a lack of intimacy. Weakness cannot support any weight. Weakness fails and stumbles, but strength is powerful. It can carry the world, and it can endure temptations and verbal attacks. Strength is gasoline for the journey; strength is your destination-fuel. It will get you where you need to go, which is why I am growing your God-muscles. What is a God-muscle? It is everything about Me that gives you strength. Truth, faithfulness, kindness, and a heart of forgiveness are God-muscles. Every muscle of Mine makes you as strong as I am, so exercise your God-muscles! Lift the weights that make you strong. Be honest, tell the truth, be forgiving when others hurt you, be good to the unkind, and pray for those who don't like you. Grow your love-muscles; they are the strongest of all. With all My muscles you can carry the weight of the world and never feel it. There will be no weakness in you, no failure or falling apart. I give you only victory, strength, and joy for the journey. There will be no wearing out. Your strength is your water—now drink all you want—I have all you need!

Memory Verse

But people who do right will continue to do right. And those whose hands are not dirty with sin will grow stronger.

—Job 17:9

Discussion Questions

1. What is "strength"?

2. How do I grow God-muscles?

3. Why are love-muscles the strongest?

4. Discuss people and things that give us strength.

5. What are the blessings of strength?

6. What is it like without strength?

7. Who are people that had strength in the Bible?

I Am Your Armor

The night is almost gone; the day of salvation will soon be here. So remove your dark deeds like dirty clothes, and put on the shining armor of right living.

—Romans 13:12, NLT

A soldier without armor can be wounded. A soldier without armor is easily defeated, but a well-armored soldier is invincible. My armor is bullet-proof, hate-proof, rejection-proof, and failure-proof. It can deflect the bombs of jealousy, the missiles of strife, and the knives of cruelty. My armor is life-proof armor, made to fit you perfectly. It will never break or crack; it is invincible armor. Wear this armor every day. It works by love, faith, and obedience: when you love, it turns on, when you obey, it deflects arrows and spears, and when you walk by faith, it cannot be pierced. I am your Armor. I am unbreakable and impenetrable. I am invincible. When you wear Me, you are protected. You cannot lose or be defeated. Nothing evil can reach you; safe and sound, you are sheltered forever. Never leave the house without your God-armor. Every battle you will fight is already won— as long as you wear My armor. Remember, victory, safety, and power are yours when you are safe inside My armor!

Memory Verse

Wear the full armor of God. Wear God's armor so that you can fight against the devil's evil tricks.

—Ephesians 6:11

Discussion Questions

1. What is invincibility?

_____

_____

2. What makes me invincible?

_____

_____

3. Who are people that were invincible in the Bible?

_____

_____

4. How do I put on my armor?

_____

_____

5. What are the blessings of wearing God's armor?

_____

_____

6. What is the source of invincibility?

_____

_____

7. Why do I need to be invincible?

_____

_____

No Holes in Your Pockets

You have planted much but harvest little. You eat but are not satisfied. You drink but are still thirsty. You put on clothes but cannot keep warm. Your wages disappear as though you were putting them in pockets filled with holes!

—Haggai 1:6, NLT

Everything I give you is a holy treasure. Every lesson of life is an anchor for your boat. Every revealed truth is a weapon of grace. Every thought of wisdom is a foundation of power. When I give you something, I make it indestructible and eternal; all of My gifts are pieces of eternity for you. You will never be poor in Me, with Me, through Me. You are divine wealth walking. You are unhindered victory talking. Everything I give you will last forever—your family, your ministry, and your blessings. There are no holes in your pockets; no blessing can evaporate in My hands, and no joy can diminish in My will. My plan for your life is perfect. Everything your heart will ever need is already provided. Remember, there are no holes in your pockets—I guarantee it!

Memory Verse

Take delight in the Lord, and he will give you your heart's desires. Commit everything you do to the Lord. Trust him, and he will help you.

—Psalm 37:4-5, NLT

Discussion Questions

1. What is prosperity?

_____

_____

2. Who needs prosperity? Why?

_____

_____

3. Why do God's blessings last for eternity?

_____

_____

4. How do people get holes in their pockets?

_____

_____

5. Who are people that were prosperous in the Bible?

_____

_____

6. What are the blessings of prosperity?

_____

_____

7. How is God my source of prosperity?

_____

_____

Superman's Booth

And God is able to bless you abundantly, so that in all things at all times, having all that you need, you will abound in every good work.

—2 Corinthians 9:8, NIV

I can change anything, anyone, at any time. I am like Superman's booth—you go in ordinary and come out supernatural. Every transformation will lead you to a destiny. Every adjustment will bring some new happiness to your life. I love you unconditionally, just the way you are. But to use you, I must perfect you. And like a watch, you must keep time with Me. Therefore, miraculous changes will always be a part of your life. Trust Me and give Me time, and in every part of your life I will attach a transformation. Be ready for whatever you could change into. Release your Superman life: your ability to fly, not just walk, your ability to see through walls, to hear the heartbeat of people around you, and to do impossible, wonderful, life-changing feats. No one who lives for Me can stay unchanged. There is always hope where there is change. No part of you is unchangeable when you step into Me—I am Superman's booth. You go in normal but come out special. Yes, "special" is your secret word, for you are My wonderful child, touched by love's power, saved by faith's victory, and changed by Jesus Himself. Sacrifice for love, and always hope, always believe, and always trust that I can add or remove anything to make you more like Me. Relax and step into the booth!

Memory Verse

...We all show the Lord's glory, and we are being changed to be like him. This change in us brings more and more glory. And it comes from the Lord...

—2 Corinthians 3:18

Discussion Questions

1. What is "transformation"?

2. Why do I need transformation?

3. How do I keep in time with God?

4. Who was transformed in the Bible?

5. What are the blessings of transformation?

6. What are some Godly habits that bring transformation?

7. What does God think about transformation?

Why I Chose You

You made my whole being. You formed me in my mother's body. I praise you because you made me in an amazing and wonderful way. What you have done is wonderful. I know this very well.

—Psalm 139:13-14

I chose you because I formed you inside your mother's womb. I knew you were going to be a unique, gifted, wonder-worker, and a life-genius—someone that makes Me proud. I love every little detail about you. I love your heart, your mind, and your personality. I love the sound of your voice, the way you laugh, and how you care about your friends. I chose you because you chose Me. I know who you will become, and how you will change the world. You're like a river of gold, priceless and ever-flowing. You're like an ocean of untracked beauty. You remind Me of My Son, Jesus: kind, tender, loyal, honest, and gentle. I choose you every day; I choose you because I can trust you to love Me and do My will for your life. Why did I choose you? It's because you light up My life. You bring happiness to everyone who knows you, and you are a healer of lonely hearts; you repair with your unbiased love, and you make everyone feel welcomed. I could never "unchoose" you. I have chosen you now, tomorrow, and forever.

Memory Verse

...God chose you to tell about the wonderful things he has done. He called you out of darkness into his wonderful light.

—1 Peter 2:9

Discussion Questions

1. What is special about election?

_____

_____

2. Who were elected or chosen in the Bible?

_____

_____

3. Why was I elected?

_____

_____

4. Discuss how God is the Elector.

_____

_____

5. How does God know what I will become?

_____

_____

6. What are the blessings of election?

_____

_____

7. Does God "unchoose" me if I sin?

_____

_____

I Hear You Even When You Don't Talk

Then he continued, "Do not be afraid, Daniel. Since the first day that you set your mind to gain understanding and to humble yourself before your God, your words were heard, and I have come in response to them."

—Daniel 10:12, NIV

Do you know that I love you so much that I hear you even when you don't speak? You are a living letter of love to Me. You don't have to say a word, and I can still hear what you're saying. I can hear you praying even when you sleep; that's why you have so many wonderful blessings in your life—I put them there. I have heard you pray in the silence. Your prayers open My heart like a can opener. Every time you breathe, I listen. I hear silence as well as words. I am making your life a prayer for the world. First comes the prayer, then the answer—you. Yes, you are being formed into a living answer. Your life will answer people's questions about Me. Your life shall be a light in the dark, a cloud of refreshing rain for the thirsty traveler. You are My answer; I am investing all I have and all I am into you. You will never have a day where I do not make your life into a warmth like sunshine and a joy to the world. Now sit still and know that I am God, the One who hears you even when you don't speak!

Memory Verse

I will provide for their needs before they ask. I will help them while they are still asking for help.

—Isaiah 65:24

Discussion Questions

1. How does God pay attention?

_____

_____

2. Why should I give my attention to God?

_____

_____

3. Who paid attention in the Bible?

_____

_____

4. How will my life become an answer for people?

_____

_____

5. Why does God love attention?

_____

_____

6. What are the blessings of attention?

_____

_____

7. How has God invested all He is into me?

_____

_____

I Am Your Fiery Chariot

Elijah and Elisha were still walking and talking. Then a chariot and horses of fire appeared. The chariot and horses of fire separated Elijah from Elisha. Then Elijah went up to heaven in a whirlwind.

—2 Kings 2:11

Separations and uncomfortable events of life may try to get you discouraged, but look up at the fiery chariot that's headed your way. I have made you a chariot of fiery purpose, one made so perfectly for you that you will want to ride in it every day. Purpose is your daily food; it's why you were born, where you are going, and what you are going to achieve. How do you know this gift of purpose is My will for you? The chariot can only be driven by you, for no one else can drive it, and no one else understands this chariot of purpose and how you fit perfectly in it. It's yours and yours alone. I made it so it will respond to only your voice and hear only your heart. You can even get in now and stay in. Never get out of your chariot of purpose, for it will never fail you. It will always take you to places where I am waiting for you, Heavenly and sacred places, where My Presence waits with open arms. Drive it, show it off, and let everyone know that I have one for them, too. I have prepared their very own chariots of purpose also, which answer all of life's questions. They burn with the fires of joy, faith, and truth, and are crowned with love. What a life you are driving into! Now rest, call down from Heaven your chariot of purpose, and always, always set your eyes on Me, your destination!

Memory Verse

"I have good plans for you. I don't plan to hurt you. I plan to give you hope and a good future."

—Jeremiah 29:11

Discussion Questions

1. What is my fiery chariot?

_____

_____

2. How does God empower me?

_____

_____

3. Who were empowered in the Bible? For what purpose?

_____

_____

4. What are some habits for an empowered life?

_____

_____

5. In what ways am I empowered for my purpose?

_____

_____

6. Why do I need to be empowered?

_____

_____

7. How do I find my purpose?

_____

_____

I Am Making Your Sword

And take the sword of the Spirit—that sword is the teaching of God.
—Ephesians 6:17

All warriors need a sword, and I have made one just for you. You see, you are My young Swordmaster. I am training you to fight with it every day. You never want to go into battle without your Sword. Your Sword is My gift to you. When you use it, you will be protected. This Sword is mighty because it is made of pieces of Me. I live inside the Sword, and My voice comes from it. My face can be seen when you use your Sword, and it can set the prisoners free. It can cut down an entire forest of lies and dig up rocks of hardness. It pulls out the roots of deception and stumps of stubbornness; it can burn down a world of trash-thoughts and harmful ideas. This Sword will work in your hand; it will not work for a stranger. I have engraved your name on the handle of the Sword. When you use it, everything and everyone that loves Me stands at attention and listens to the sound of this sacred warrior's Sword. Many enemies of Mine have been defeated and converted by it. It is My power in your hand—now use it! Liberate the slaves of the world. Break every chain and free every captive!

Memory Verse

For the word of God is alive and active. Sharper than any double-edged sword...it judges the thoughts and attitudes of the heart.

—Hebrews 4:12, NIV

Discussion Questions

1. Who in the Bible was trained? How?

2. Why do I need to be trained?

3. How do I use my sword?

4. Can I be trained both for good and bad?

5. What are the blessings of Godly training?

6. What are the habits of training?

7. How do I go to battle?

I Am Never Mad at You

But Lord, you are a God who shows mercy and is kind. You don't become angry quickly. You have great love and faithfulness.

—Psalm 86:15

When My Son Jesus saved you, He removed all My anger from ever approaching you. You see, I am never mad at you. So don't be mad at yourself, for anger burns out My love, it steals My peace, and it creates a wrong destiny. Anger is the Devil's food, trying to poison you, so always reject it! Be like Me; I am never mad at you. I already know what you're going to do before you do it. I know you will love Me, follow Me, and serve Me first in your life. As you grow, I will grow My love inside you and teach you how to heal the hurting. I will show you the secrets of bringing hope to the discouraged and how to multiply My happiness to the lost souls of this world. Why? Because I am never mad at you, I believe in you. I believe in your future. I trust Myself in you. I have already loved you all your life. Love is your trumpet, your message for the people around you. Be like Me. Love them when they expect you to be mad at them, and they will know I am not mad at them either.

Memory Verse

O Lord, you are so good, so ready to forgive,
so full of unfailing love for all who ask for your help.

—**Psalm 86:5, NLT**

Discussion Questions

1. What is forgiveness?

_____

_____

2. How did Jesus remove God's anger?

_____

_____

3. What are the habits of forgiveness?

_____

_____

4. Why does God forgive?

_____

_____

5. Why should we forgive?

_____

_____

6. Why should I forgive myself?

_____

_____

7. Why does God believe in my future?

_____

_____

WK 37: CELEBRATION

I Am Always Clapping for You

So he returned home to his father. And while he was still a long way off, his father saw him coming. Filled with love and compassion, he ran to his son, embraced him, and kissed him.

—Luke 15:20, NLT

I am so pleased with you that I am clapping for you. Even before you run any race or take any journey, I am already rejoicing. I think you are amazing! You are so wonderful and so full of potential that I will clap it out of you. I will celebrate the greatness in you until it comes out. I will rejoice over you and release your victories. Your miracle life is coming. Every time I clap, your next miracle happens to you. Every time something good happens, know that I am celebrating you! You are not bad, you are not useless, and you are not broken or damaged. Those that have hurt you are not stronger than I am. I am the Antidote to life. I am the Cure for all bad people, bad days, and unexplainable circumstances. Trust Me with all your heart, and you will begin to hear the thousands of angels and people that are now clapping for you with Me!

Memory Verse

...there will be more rejoicing in heaven over one sinner who repents than over ninety-nine righteous persons who do not need to repent.

—Luke 15:7, NIV

Discussion Questions

1. What is "celebration"?

_____

_____

2. Who does God celebrate?

_____

_____

3. Who should we celebrate?

_____

_____

4. Why does God celebrate people?

_____

_____

5. What fruit comes from a life of celebration?

_____

_____

6. How can I create a life of celebration?

_____

_____

7. Why do we need to celebrate others?

_____

_____

Look Around You

Religion that God the Father accepts is this: caring for orphans or widows who need help; and keeping yourself free from the world's evil influence. This is the kind of religion that God accepts as pure and good.

—James 1:27

You are My rescuer. You were born to help the helpless. You have special life-saving gifts and they are waiting to be released. They merely wait for the sound of your voice. When you say "yes" to Me, they wake up. These are your compassion gifts. They will lead you to the helpless, hopeless orphans of the world. Your compassion gifts love, cherish and heal the heart of helpless. You are My orphan-rescuer, My widow-deliverer, My poor man's feeder. You will always be important to Me, and I will always have a purpose for you. Look around you every day and I will show you where to go, whom to help, and how to help them. Stretch out your hand and touch someone's heart, My amazing rescuer!

Memory Verse

Learn to do good. Seek justice. Help the oppressed. Defend the cause of orphans. Fight for the rights of widows.

—Isaiah 1:17, NLT

Discussion Questions

1. What is compassion?

_____

_____

2. How do I have compassion gifts? Why?

_____

_____

3. Who in the Bible showed compassion?

_____

_____

4. Why is it pure to take care of orphans and widows?

_____

_____

5. How does God lead me?

_____

_____

6. Who in my life could I show more compassion to?

_____

_____

7. What are the blessings of compassion?

_____

_____

I Never Laugh at You

The Lord loves us very much.
His truth is everlasting.
Praise the Lord!

—Psalm 117:2

Everything about you is beautiful, and there are no ugly pieces of you. You are My perfectly-made miracle. Yes, YOU. You may ask me, "Why?" The reason: you are going to change the world! I mean it, though others who do not know you may laugh. Sometimes, others laugh because they are afraid or because no one loves them. Other times, it's because someone is laughing at them. Only agree with My love for you, and someday they will understand and will laugh with you. Your destiny is to be like My beautiful love and healing music on earth. Cruel and careless laughter has wounded their hearts, and your mission will be to sing their wounds away. You are My healing music. I am already proud of you for the way you will care for those that no one wants and help those with no family. I sing over you songs filled with light and joy, and with these songs, you will always make the dark shadows flee away from those who are hurting. Laugh, rejoice, dance freely, and smile with Me because I smile over you.

Memory Verse

You have also given me the shield of Your salvation;
Your right hand has held me up,
Your gentleness has made me great.

—Psalm 18:35, NKJV

Discussion Questions

1. What is identity?

2. Who in the Bible found their identity?

3. Why do I need to know my identity?

4. How can I agree with God's love for me and not what others say?

5. Why is God already proud of me?

6. How do I feel God smiling over me?

7. Who are people around me that know their identity?

your special Net

*Simon answered, "Master, we worked hard all night trying to catch
fish, but we caught nothing. But you say to put the nets in the water;
so I will." The fishermen did as Jesus told them. And they caught so
many fish that the nets began to break.*

—Luke 5:5-6

Let's go fishing! Oh, we are about to catch some big fish, so big that
they have escaped all of the other fishermen. These fish have been
waiting for you, and they won't come into anyone else's net but
yours. I have made this net especially for you; no one else can use
it but you and you alone. Do you see how big the ocean is, how vast
and wide? Out there in the loneliness of that ocean are the fish that
belong to Me. Because I love them, I need and want them with Me.
I am praying for them because I don't want them to be lost or eaten
by other fish. Some fish have no mercy and no love—only hunger.
Therefore, they need us to catch them. You see, fish are the people
who are lost, people swimming in darkness, just waiting for us. Let's
catch them in My net made of love, mercy, and truth. Let's take the
net and cast it into the sea. I know with confidence that you are
an expert fisherman of Mine; yes, your net will never break or rot,
because it is made of Me, for Me, through you. The fish are coming.
The fish are here! Now pick up your net and let's bring these
fish home!

Memory Verse

Then He said to them, "Follow Me, and I will make you fishers of men."

—Matthew 4:19, NKJV

Discussion Questions

1. What is evangelism?

_____

_____

2. Why should I be an evangelist?

_____

_____

3. What are the blessings of evangelism?

_____

_____

4. Where does evangelism happen?

_____

_____

5. What are the habits for successfully catching fish?

_____

_____

6. What does God think about evangelism?

_____

_____

7. Why does the world need evangelism?

_____

_____

You Are My Explorer

The Lord said to Moses, "Send men to explore the land of Canaan. I will give that land to the Israelites. Send one leader from each tribe."

—Numbers 13:1-2

Let's go exploring! Let's climb the highest mountain, all the way to the top, from which we can see into eternity. Let's put on our exploring boots, which can climb any mountain without slipping and can cross any river without sinking. Yes, you are My explorer. I created you to discover the mysteries of the world. I have planned hundreds of adventures for us. We will scale mountains, cross rivers, and fly into the sky. We will find the lost and hidden treasures of life together. Let's explore, for I have things to show you that I have never shown anyone before! I will show you the hidden mysteries of science, nature, animals, plants, oceans, chemicals, soils, fruits, fishes, and the stars. I already own everything you can see, and anything I own, you own. It's all there for the discovering, ready and waiting to appear. Nothing is off limits to you; I am offering it all. Let's go now; put on your boots and let's explore My universe!

Memory Verse

"So go to the street corners and invite everyone you see. Tell them to come to my feast."

—Matthew 22:9

Discussion Questions

1. What is an exploration-heart?

2. How do I explore God?

3. How do I explore God's Word?

4. Why do I need an exploration-heart?

5. What are the blessings of exploration?

6. Who were explorers in the Bible?

7. How does exploration require faith and bravery?

My House Is Your House

I ask only one thing from the Lord. This is what I want: Let me live in the Lord's house all my life. Let me see the Lord's beauty. Let me look around in his Temple.

—Psalm 27:4

My house is your house. I built it just for you—your home, with your own room, with all your favorite things in it. All the things and all the people who love Me are in My house. My house is a very happy place. There is no sickness, no death, no hurt, and no pain. No one who comes to My house ever wants to leave. It is never cold. There are no rats, no spiders, no snakes, and no dangerous people. My house cannot break, be burnt down, or be blown away. This house, which is yours also, will last forever. In My house, no one is ever bored, angry, or sad. There are rooms for all the people you love—your family, your best friends, and all of your animals. In My house it's never dark, you never get tired, and you never feel afraid. Relax, lie down, rest! You're in My house, our house, and you never have to leave. It's all yours—forever and ever and ever. Now get ready to invite some more people into our house!

Memory Verse

*Surely your goodness and love will be with me
all my life. And I will live in the house of the Lord forever.*

—Psalm 23:6

Discussion Questions

1. What are the blessings of a family?

_____

_____

2. What is special about being in God's house?

_____

_____

3. How can I show my family that I love them?

_____

_____

4. How does God make His home in me?

_____

_____

5. How can I invite others into God's family?

_____

_____

6. Discuss what a blessed family looks like.

_____

_____

7. How does God outwork His purpose through family?

_____

_____

Blow Your Trumpet

Blow the trumpet and shout, 'Long live King Solomon!'

—1 Kings 1:34

I have a choice trumpet, made especially for you. No one else can play it; if they try, it makes no sound. Your trumpet only plays for you. Your trumpet is for playing the sounds that make the whole world sing for Me. You cannot make sad sounds, miserable noises, or fearful squeaks—it is the trumpet of freedom. It sets the prisoners free and breaks the chains of unhappiness. Blow your trumpet; sound it loud, and let the whole universe hear it! Anyone who hears this trumpet is automatically freed; but if no one plays it, then no one can be released. You are My Holy Releaser. Oh, the beautiful sounds we will make together! It will always make sorrow flee away, pain melt, trouble die, and fear vanish like a puff of smoke. The secret is that the trumpet is your assignment from Me; the trumpet is Me. Tell everyone about Me, and they will hear and come close. They were made to hear the sound of My voice exactly when they need it most. Now pick up your trumpet and blow the other sounds away! Let the world hear the sound of happiness!

Memory Verse

The Lord says, "Shout out loud. Don't hold back.
Shout out loud like a trumpet..."

—Isaiah 58:1

Discussion Questions

1. What is "assignment"?

_____

_____

2. Why does God assign me a destiny?

_____

_____

3. How do I become a blessing-assignment for others?

_____

_____

4. When will God assign me a destiny?

_____

_____

5. Discuss different ways that I can play my trumpet.

_____

_____

6. How do I discover God's assignment for me?

_____

_____

7. What are the blessings of assignment?

_____

_____

Let's Go Treasure Hunting

And in him all the treasures of wisdom and knowledge are safely kept.

—Colossians 2:3

What are your favorite things? You know a few, but I know them all—everything you like and love, everything you enjoy. I know it all, and I have also kept some surprises for you. I have laid up for you things so wonderful that they are not made on Earth. These treasures are Heavenly treasures. They are made by the angels and beautifully covered in Heavenly wrapping paper, which doesn't tear or wrinkle. Your treasures are kept in My special treasure chest which is full of your dreams. You see, your dreams are the makers of your treasures. They decide what you like and dislike. Know this: these treasures multiply every time you obey Me. Every time you say "yes" to My will, a new treasure appears. I love giving you new presents and surprise treasures. I love hearing you laugh with joy, and I love when you thank Me and praise Me and sing to Me. These are the treasures you give to Me. They're like candy to me; I save every prayer of yours in the treasure chest of Heaven. Every "thank you" is a song, every "I love you" is a miracle, and every praise is a thunderous applause. All of us here in Heaven can't wait to give you something you can enjoy forever to sing and dance and laugh about. Okay, now the treasure chest is yours—let's fill it together!

Memory Verse

The blessing of the Lord makes one rich,
And He adds no sorrow with it.

—Proverbs 10:22, NKJV

Discussion Questions

1. What is a reward?

_____

_____

2. Why does God reward obedience?

_____

_____

3. Why does a new treasure appear when I obey God?

_____

_____

4. What are the richest rewards?

_____

_____

5. How do my dreams make my treasures?

_____

_____

6. How can I become a rewarder?

_____

_____

7. What are God's rewards for me?

_____

_____

Good Friends Are a Gift of Love

A friend loves you all the time.
A brother is always there to help you.

—Proverbs 17:17

I will always be your Best Friend, because, after all, only I can move through space and time, occupying all of creation. I am never away from you. I stay closer than close; I am your constant companion and friend. You can always be sure that I hear you every time you call. I feel you when you hurt, and I come to you when you need Me. Never doubt that I am there watching over you, making sure you're okay. In Me you are protected, covered, healthy, warm, comforted, answered, defined, and assigned. I can never forget you, though others may; I'm always on a love-assignment with you. Be happy and make others happy! Tell them Who I am and what I'm like. This is your assignment; this is your calling. Build your character. Grow into someone who is kind, generous, loyal, and trustworthy. Don't just reward people who give you something. Become a kind friend to all. Be a friend to the friendless and light to those who live in darkness. I am with you. My truth is your light, and your light is your medicine. Now grow, and become a best friend to the poor and needy!

Memory Verse

Some friends may ruin you. But a real friend will be more loyal than a brother.

—Proverbs 18:24

Discussion Questions

1. What is "character"?

_____

_____

2. What is God's character like?

_____

_____

3. How is God my best friend?

_____

_____

4. How does having character bless others?

_____

_____

5. How do I develop character?

_____

_____

6. Who showed true friendship in the Bible?

_____

_____

7. How can I be a true friend?

_____

_____

Truth-Soap

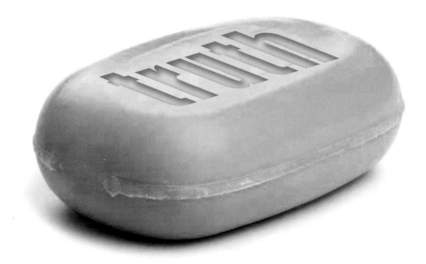

Jesus answered, "I am the way. And I am the truth and the life. The only way to the Father is through me."

—John 14:6

I remove all of the guilt-dirt and wash away all of the shame-slime. You are forgiven, I accept you, and you are My favorite child. Therefore, whenever you feel like you're far away from Me, remember to wash yourself with truth-soap. Lies are like Satan's poison eggs—they promise, but they never deliver; they create a false, fake image of the future. All lies, all sins, and all falsehoods smear mud and dirt on the windows of your soul. Take your truth-soap with you everywhere you go. Never leave home without it! It will save you many miles of bad directions. It will allow you to hear Me with unclogged ears; it will make your eyes see with no danger of losing focus. This truth-soap can both kill and wash away every lie. It is where I live. I live in the truth but never in a lie. The world is full of lies—but I am Truth. Use Me on them and become a lie-cleanser and a falsehood-exposer. Always tell the truth and you will never feel dirty, muddy, or unclean. Truth sets you free. It makes Me trust you, and I only use those I can trust. Now use your truth soap and clean the world!

Memory Verse

Then you will know the truth. And the truth will make you free.
—John 8:32

Discussion Questions

1. What is honesty?

2. How does honesty bring a richness to life?

3. Why does God love honesty?

4. Who are honest people in my life?

5. What are some worldly lies?

6. How do I wash in truth-soap?

7. Why should I love honesty?

New clothes for you

The Lord makes me very happy. All that I am rejoices in my God. The Lord has covered me with clothes of salvation. He has covered me with a coat of goodness. I am like a bridegroom dressed for his wedding. I am like a bride dressed in jewels.

—Isaiah 61:10

As you grow, your clothes will change. As you build your faith-muscles, you will need new shirts, new pants, and new shoes. I know exactly what fits you. If your clothes are too small, then they will tear; if they are too big, they will hang loosely on you and cause you to trip. But if I design them, they will fit perfectly. Your clothes are your destiny-tools: your gifts, anointings, virtues, and habits. Consider them like a pair of shoes—they are the instruments that will carry you to your best looking, best feeling, and best fitted life. Never dislike your God-clothes. They never wrinkle, wear out, or tear. They are made from only the best materials—the everlasting materials of unconditional love, unbiased truth, perfect patience, mercy, grace, kindness, praise, compassion, and forgiveness. Love your clothes and they will always fit—making you all that I want you to be. But you have to dress in My clothes and My divine materials for a divine you. I love you, and I love you enough to supply everything you'll ever need. So smile, and grow into your God-clothes!

Memory Verse

Seek the Kingdom of God above all else, and live righteously, and he will give you everything you need.

—Matthew 6:33, NLT

Discussion Questions

1. What is an adjustment?

2. How do I put on God's new clothes?

3. Why should I be adjustable?

4. What are God-clothes made out of?

5. How do I know what I should adjust?

6. What adjustments could I make now?

7. Why does God love it when people are adjustable?

Sharing is Caring

The person who gives to the poor will have everything he needs. But the one who ignores the poor will have many curses put on him.

—Proverbs 28:27

I love you so much. In fact, I have so much love that I gave My Son for all those who hate Me. I sent Him to rescue all people, even those who will never accept and love Me. I am a giver and a sharer. Sharing is caring—after all; anyone can take other people's things or keep what they have for themselves. Everyone knows this, but I am making you a giver. Why? I do this so that you will never lack anything you need. You see, the more you give, the more I will send you. If you spend your life giving to others, I will spend My life giving to you. Open your hands and give away those things that you really like; every time you give away something precious or valuable, your heart grows and makes more room for something new. Sharing is caring. Those that share look like Me. Those that share are as rich as I am, for those who give will always have My provision; they will never be poor. Be a sharer, a giver, and a blessing to those who have nothing. Remember, I own everything, and you belong to Me. Now grow into your giving shoes!

Memory Verse

Give, and you will receive. You will be given much...The way you give to others is the way God will give to you.

—Luke 6:38

Discussion Questions

1. What is generosity?

_____

_____

2. Who was generous in the Bible?

_____

_____

3. What does sharing do for others?

_____

_____

4. Who can I be more generous toward?

_____

_____

5. What are the habits of generosity?

_____

_____

6. What are the blessings of generosity?

_____

_____

7. Why does God give more to generous people?

_____

_____

I Love Donkeys

The donkey saw the angel of the Lord. So she lay down under Balaam. Balaam was very angry and hit her with his stick. Then the Lord made the donkey talk. She said to Balaam, "What have I done to make you hit me three times?"

—**Numbers 22:27-28**

Balaam sat upon his donkey; he whipped and screamed and yelled at her, but Balaam did not know that I had sent this donkey to save his life. Sometimes, people only see what's on the outside; they only see the strange ways people look, talk, or walk, but I love donkeys. I love anyone who is unique, different, and gifted, because I know that I can place My voice, My wisdom, and My solution inside of them. Balaam would have lost his way and lost his head if he had not listened to his donkey. Always nurture, cherish, and love those who are different. Show mercy to them, for I will use them in divine ways to change the world. They may look like ugly, weird, useless donkeys, but they can walk through places that others cannot. They can carry heavy loads and burdens. They can walk on dangerous cliffs and never get tired or afraid. They are loyal and determined, and they see and feel in a way that others do not. Yes, these are My donkeys; they are special, so love them. Help them and show them the way to Me. Now grow into your donkey-loving shoes!

Memory Verse

The Lord is not slow in doing what he promised...God is being patient with you...He wants everyone to change his heart and life.

—2 Peter 3:9

Discussion Questions

1. What is mercy?

_____

_____

2. Who had mercy in the Bible?

_____

_____

3. Why should I be merciful?

_____

_____

4. How can I look inside someone and see their value?

_____

_____

5. How do I become a donkey-lover?

_____

_____

6. In what ways am I a donkey?

_____

_____

7. To whom can I show more mercy?

_____

_____

I Can, You Can

But the Lord said to me, "My grace is enough for you. When you are weak, then my power is made perfect in you." So I am very happy to brag about my weaknesses. Then Christ's power can live in me.

—2 Corinthians 12:9

Say, "I can!" because all your life you will be a champion for the "I can't" people of the world. When life's challenges come, and you feel you've reached your limits, remember to say out loud to yourself, "I can do this—I can conquer every mountain. I can love every enemy. I can learn every lesson. I can see the truth no matter what anyone is saying. I can change. I can rise above my problems. I can be what God wants me to be. I can, I can, I can ALWAYS say 'yes' to my destiny. I can change the world. I can dream the biggest dreams and climb the highest mountains!" In Me, you certainly can. Let Me remove your fears, doubts, and self-consciousness. Become God-conscious. My Word has been spoken over your life, and I will fulfill it. Find your confidence in Me, for I have filled you with Myself. I live in you, so know that if I can, you can. Now grow into your "I cans"!

Memory Verse

I can do all things through Christ because he gives me strength.
—Philippians 4:13

Discussion Questions

1. What is "confidence"?

_____

_____

2. Who had confidence in the Bible?

_____

_____

3. How do I place my confidence in God?

_____

_____

4. How does talking out loud to myself affect my outcome?

_____

_____

5. What are habits that develop confidence?

_____

_____

6. What are some things God has spoken over my life?

_____

_____

7. Why can I do what God has for me?

_____

_____

Loaves and Fishes

"Here is a boy with five loaves of barley bread and two little fish. But that is not enough for so many people." Jesus said, "Tell the people to sit down." This was a very grassy place. There were about 5,000 men who sat down there. Then Jesus took the loaves of bread. He thanked God for the bread and gave it to the people who were sitting there. He did the same with the fish. He gave them as much as they wanted. They all had enough to eat. When they had finished, Jesus said to His followers, "Gather the pieces of fish and bread that were not eaten. Don't waste anything." So they gathered up the pieces that were left. They filled 12 large baskets with the pieces that were left of the five barley loaves.

—John 6:9-13

Even if you give Me just a little, that can become more than enough. Bring Me your loaves and fish, and watch Me multiply everything you have. One loaf will become one thousand loaves; one fish will feed a town, a state, and a nation. All I need is your faith and trust, and I will do the rest. You will experience no lack. I am offering you total supply. Never think that you don't have enough. Remember, I am more than enough, more than you need. I fill the hunger in people's stomachs and their hearts, and I give you the power to raise the poor out of the dust and trash heaps of the world. I give you the resources to live out your dreams and reach your destiny. Never ever look back; only the desert lies behind you. Scorpions, snakes, and rats live there. Look ahead and show Me those loaves, and give Me those fish!

Memory Verse

With God's power working in us, God can do much, much more than anything we can ask or think of.

—Ephesians 3:20

Discussion Questions

1. What is provision?

_____

_____

2. What "loaves and fishes" in my life can I give God?

_____

_____

3. In what ways can I activate God's provision?

_____

_____

4. What are the blessings of provision?

_____

_____

5. How has God provided for me already?

_____

_____

6. How is God always more than enough for me?

_____

_____

7. How can I become a provider for others?

_____

_____

Bring Your Vessels

*Then Elisha said, "Go and get empty jars from all your neighbors.
Don't ask for just a few."*

—2 Kings 4:3

You are My vessel, My house; you are My dwelling place. I live in
you all day and all night. I draw you to Me with love, and I have
something to give you. But it's too big for you to carry, so go get your
vessels, pots, and barrels, because I will fill them with power, mercy,
wisdom, victory, tolerance, and self-worth. Create empty places for
Me to fill. How much do you want? You name it; I'll supply it. Call on
Me and I'll pour the blessings into your vessels. Every pot will brim
full of joys, miracles, and surprises. So never doubt My generosity;
never question My good intentions. My gifts are always good, and I
have many for you! You will become a filler of the empty-hearted, a
supplier for the poorest of the poor, a need-meeter, a burden-lifter, a
caregiver, and a light-shiner. Come now, and bring as many vessels as
you can. There is no such thing as too many. Everything I have
is yours.

Memory Verse

For the good of his name, he leads me on paths that are right. Even if I walk through a very dark valley, I will not be afraid because you are with me.

—Psalm 23:3-4

Discussion Questions

1. How do I create empty places?

2. What is willingness?

3. Why should I be a willing vessel?

4. How do I get a willing heart?

5. What are the blessings of willingness?

6. How does God fill my pots?

7. Who are three people who were willing in the Bible?

COME

Casa Angelina hosts teams most months each year.

TO

Our children are always very excited to see them!

GUATEMALA...

Teams work at our mountainside orphan community,

WHATMATTERSMM.ORG/GO

and connect with our beautiful children and widows.